CLIMATE CHANGE

IN

OCEAN HABITAT

STEPH NORIS

COPYRIGHT

Copyright © 2021 by STEPH NORIS: All rights reserved. This book or any portion thereof may not be reproduced or used in any manner whatsoever without the express written permission of the author except for the use of brief quotations in a book review.

TABLE OF CONTENTS

INTRODUCTION 4

CHAPTER 1 6

OCEAN HABITAT 6

CHAPTER 2 8

MAJOR CAUSES OF CLIMATE CHANGE 8

CHAPTER 3 12

CLIMATE CHANGE IN THE OCEAN 12

CHAPTER 4 15

OCEAN ATMOSPHERE 15

CHAPTER 5 18

SOLVING THE OCEAN'S CLIMATE PROBLEM 18

CHAPTER 6 21

CLIMATE CHANGE AND THE OCEAN 21

CHAPTER 7 28

POLLUTION IN THE OCEAN 28

CHAPTER 8..30

PROTECTING OUR OCEAN 30

CONCLUSION 34

INTRODUCTION

The greatest diversity of life on Earth can be found in the oceans. Marine species can be found everywhere, from the Polar Regions to the tropical oceans, and deep-sea hydrothermal vents to shallow seagrass beds. Humans are reliant on the oceans for vital natural resources. Over 200 million people rely on fishing for their livelihood, and more than a billion rely on it for protein. Climate change has an impact on human health and well-being by increasing the frequency of extreme weather events and wildfires, lowering air quality, and spreading diseases through insects, food, and water.

Within the scientific community, there is widespread consensus that climate change is real. Human activity is contributing to climate change. While nearly all scientists, scientific organizations, and governments agree that climate change is occurring and is being caused by human activities, a small minority of voices reject the veracity of such declarations and choose to cast doubt on the overwhelming evidence.

Although the task of combating climate change appears daunting, solutions exist to ensure a live ocean and a healthy global environment. More than 100 countries accounting for 90% of global emissions have already committed to reducing carbon pollution at the national level. World leaders are collaborating to write the next actions to address climate change responsibly, ensuring the security and resilience of the world's most vulnerable people, places, and species. This book serves as a roadmap for how we can take the steps necessary to save our world.

We can safeguard the ocean habitat, as well as the many species and communities that rely on it if we work together.

CHAPTER 1
OCEAN HABITAT

Water covers over three-quarters of the Earth's surface, earning it the nickname "Blue Planet." The changing chemistry of ocean water, combined with other pressures like overfishing and pollution, is causing changes in marine-based food supply and causing harm to fishing communities. Ecosystems such as forests, barrier beaches, and wetlands are losing their ability to buffer the effects of catastrophic events such as fires, floods, and severe storms. There are habitats or locations in the water where plants and animals have adapted to live within each ecosystem. The ocean is the largest biome on the planet. Oceans are changing in a variety of ways due to overexploitation of fish and other resources, destructive fishing, unregulated development, pollution, and climate change. Even in isolated regions, such as the middle of the Pacific, where plastic rubbish accumulates, human impacts can be observed.

Oceans are a universal force of nature that constitute the bedrock of the blue world we call home. They span 71 percent of our planet's surface and account for 95 percent of all living space. They are a life-support system for the Earth, providing us with free commodities and services ranging from food to oxygen. The oceans also play a role in global climate regulation, regulating temperature and driving weather patterns such as rainfall, droughts, and floods. They are also the world's largest carbon store, with marine waters accounting for roughly 83 percent of the global carbon cycle.

From glaciers to tropical reefs, there are many distinct types of environments and plant and animal groups. A biome is a huge geographical region with its own climate, geology, and oceanography. Each biome has its own collection of habitats and biodiversity. Shallow, sunny, and warm ecosystems exist. Others are dark, frigid, and deep. Plant and animal species can adapt to a variety of habitat variables, including water velocity, light intensity, temperature, water pressure, nutrients, food availability, and water salinity. Species that live in ocean and coastal ecosystems can help to develop them. The eco-engineers of the coasts are corals, kelp, mangroves, salt marshes, and seagrasses. They alter the marine environment in order to provide a home for other organisms. Coastal and open ocean habitats are the two types of ocean ecosystems. Even though coastal habitats on the continental shelf account for only 7% of the total ocean area, they are home to the majority of marine life. The majority of open ocean habitats are found beyond the continental shelf's edge in the deep ocean.

CHAPTER 2
MAJOR CAUSES OF CLIMATE CHANGE

The rise in average surface temperatures on Earth is referred to as climate change, often known as global warming. Climate change, according to scientific consensus, is mostly caused by the human use of fossil fuels, which releases carbon dioxide and other greenhouse gases into the atmosphere. The gases trap heat in the atmosphere, which can have a variety of consequences for ecosystems, such as increasing sea levels, extreme weather events, and droughts that make landscapes more vulnerable to wildfires.

The combustion of fossil fuels such as oil and coal, which generate greenhouse gases into the atmosphere, chiefly carbon dioxide, is the primary cause of climate change. Agriculture and deforestation, for example, both contribute to the accumulation of greenhouse gases that cause climate change. While several of these gases are naturally occurring and important components of the Earth's temperature management system, CO_2 concentrations in the atmosphere did not exceed 300 parts per million between the dawn of human civilization and 1900. It is currently about 400 parts per million, a level not seen in over 400,000 years. The increased use of fossil fuels has had a significant impact on climate change.

Consequences: Climate change can have serious consequences on the Earth's temperature. The average temperature of the world has risen 1.4 degrees Fahrenheit in the last century and is anticipated to rise as much as 11.5 degrees Fahrenheit in the next. Although this may not seem like much, the average temperature during the last Ice Age was around 4 degrees Fahrenheit lower than it is today. Rising sea levels due to climate change-related melting of the polar ice caps contribute to more storm damage; warmer ocean temperatures are linked to stronger and more frequent storms; more rainfall, especially during severe weather events, causes flooding and other damage; an increase in the frequency and severity of wildfires endangers habitats, homes, and lives.

Greenhouse Gas Emissions: The greenhouse effect is the primary cause of climate change. Some gases in the Earth's atmosphere act like greenhouse glass, trapping the sun's heat and preventing it from escaping into space, resulting in global warming. Many of these greenhouse gases are produced naturally, but human activity is increasing their levels in the atmosphere, especially fluorinated gases, methane, carbon dioxide (CO2), and nitrous oxide. Human-caused CO2 is the most significant contributor to global warming. Its content in the atmosphere had climbed to 48 percent above its pre-industrial level in the atmosphere by 2020, compared to 1750. Human activity also emits lower amounts of other greenhouse gases. Methane is a stronger greenhouse gas than CO2, although it has a shorter lifespan in the atmosphere. Like CO2, nitrous oxide is a long-lasting greenhouse gas that builds up in the atmosphere over decades to centuries. Between 1890 and 2010, natural processes such as variations in solar radiation or volcanic activity are estimated to have contributed less than 0.1°C to total warming.

Global Warming: Between 2011 and 2020, the world witnessed the warmest decades. In 2019, scientists reported that the global average temperature had risen 1.1 degrees Celsius over pre-industrial levels. Global warming caused by humans is currently increasing at a pace of 0.2°C per decade, indicating that we must minimize our carbon footprint. A 2°C increase in temperature relative to pre-industrial periods has major negative consequences for the natural ecosystem as well as human health and wellbeing, including a much increased likelihood of harmful and potentially catastrophic changes in the global environment.

Warming should be kept below 2°C, and efforts should be made to keep it below 1.5°C.

Emissions: Fluorinated gases are emitted by fluorinated gas-using equipment and goods. These emissions have a warming effect that is up to 23 000 times stronger than CO2. Carbon dioxide and nitrous oxide are produced when coal, oil, and gas are burned. Deforestation is the process of destroying forests. By absorbing CO2 from the atmosphere, trees assist to control the climate. When trees are cut down, the beneficial effect is gone, and the carbon contained in the trees is released into the atmosphere, so contributing to the greenhouse effect. Nitrous oxide emissions are produced by nitrogen fertilizers. Increased livestock production. When cows and sheep digest their meal, they produce a lot of methane.

CHAPTER 3
CLIMATE CHANGE IN THE OCEAN

The seas have absorbed a third of the CO2 created by human activities and 90% of the excess heat trapped by rising greenhouse gas concentrations over the last 200 years. As the climate adjusts to decades of rising carbon emissions, the ocean accumulates energy and heat from the atmosphere. If we hit a tipping point, we can expect more extreme weather, shifting ocean currents, rising sea levels and temperatures, and the melting of sea ice and ice sheets, all of which exacerbate the negative effects of overfishing, illegal fishing, pollution, and habitat destruction.

Severe storms in coastal water: Continuous CO2 absorption raises acidity levels, and when paired with global warming, more coral reefs are dying, unable to provide a healthy ocean habitat for the species that rely on them for food and protection. The heat is also affecting marine ecosystems. According to scientists, if current temperature rise rates continue, the oceans will be too warm for coral reefs by 2050. Climate change is rapidly influencing our oceans, even if we can't see it. Over the last century, the average global temperature has risen by 1.5 degrees Fahrenheit. Observable changes on land, such as the severity of wildfires, snowfall, and severe precipitation, are all part of climate change.

Oceans Are Becoming Warmer All Year: As climate change causes oceans to become warmer all year, certain species may adapt by moving to cooler places. This is harmful to fish and other marine animals. The ecosystems in which fish, shellfish, and other marine species live can be affected by changes in water temperature. Warmer oceans increase the amount of water that evaporates into the air, resulting in severe storms in coastal waters. More moisture-laden air can produce more intense precipitation when it flows over land or converges into a storm system. Heavy rain in coastal locations can increase runoff and flooding, lowering water quality when pollutants from the land wash into bodies of water. Dead zones, which are areas where water is deprived of oxygen due to pollution from agricultural fertilizers, are already present in several coastal locations, such as the Gulf of Mexico and the Chesapeake Bay. The term "dead zone" refers to an area that is devoid of life. Ocean temperatures and wind patterns are also affected by climate change, which can alter oceanic currents.

Oceans Are Becoming More Acidic: As carbon dioxide levels in the atmosphere rise as a result of human activities such as burning fossil fuels, the acidity of seawater is rising. Carbon dioxide levels are higher than they have been in the last 500,000 years. Carbon dioxide dissolves in water, affecting the chemistry of the water and lowering the pH values, making the water more acidic. Thinner shells result from increased acidity in the ocean, and more shellfish perish as predators find them easier to consume. Corals are particularly vulnerable to increased acidity because it is difficult for them to build and maintain the skeletal structures that they require for support and defence. Thousands of marine species rely on corals for spawning habitat and support.

CHAPTER 4
OCEAN ATMOSPHERE

Higher temperatures are harmful to both fish and humans. The likelihood of fewer and smaller fish in the water is bad news for the 3 billion people who rely on fish as their primary source of protein. Most fish, as well as cephalopods like octopus and squid, are affected directly by changes in water temperatures. Warmer waters may promote a mass movement of marine species in pursuit of the best feeding and spawning conditions. The implications of persistently rising temperatures on marine life are numerous. Warmer waters produce coral bleaching, which has a negative impact on coral reef ecosystems, which house the majority of the ocean's biodiversity and provide vital food supplies for humans. As the sea level rises, critical coastal ecosystems such as sea turtle breeding beaches are gone. Barriers such as cliffs, sea walls, and coastal constructions, as well as natural and man-made barriers, prevent animals from moving further inland. The same fossil fuel combustion that raises greenhouse gas levels in the atmosphere also changes the chemical composition of salt water, making it more acidic. When carbon dioxide dissolves in water and generates carbonic acid, the ocean absorbs 30% of the carbon dioxide in the atmosphere.

Rising Sea Levels: This is an unstoppable, slow-moving catastrophe. When land-based Arctic ice melts, it makes its way to the sea, posing a double threat to sea levels. When water heats, it expands to take up more space, causing the sea-level rise in an unnoticed way. Sea-level rise is currently accelerating at a rate of around one-eighth inch per year. Small island states in the Pacific Ocean, for example, are at risk of being wiped off the map as sea levels rise. The residents of Kiribati, for example, are among the world's first sea-level-rise refugees, with two of the country's islands completely submerged. Coral reefs, mangroves, sea grasses, and other species that create vital habitats rely on their capacity to travel into shallower waters to survive. Slow-growing species will almost certainly be unable to keep up with rising sea levels.

Polar Ice Is Melting: The Arctic food chain is built on the production of algae, which is dependent on the presence of sea ice. As sea ice melts, algae bloom, affecting species ranging from Arctic cod to seals, whales, and bears. Wintertime Arctic sea ice continues to plummet to new lows as the oceans warm, in what has become a depressing annual ritual. According to recent studies, Antarctica is shrinking from below due to the rapid melting of submerged ice. Antarctic krill, the food source for many seabirds and mammals in the Southern Ocean, need sea ice to survive.

Antarctic krill populations have fallen in recent years as sea ice has shrunk, resulting in decreases in krill-dependent species. Sea ice loss causes seals, walruses, penguins, whales, and other megafauna to lose essential habitat. The repercussions of Arctic cod fishing are cascading, resulting in human-wildlife conflict. Polar bears are being pushed closer to coastal villages and hunting camps by a huge drop in sea ice and seafood, which might be a nuisance and a hazard to those who live there.

Migration: The migratory patterns of marine species can shift when the currents they follow change, and many species that rely on ocean currents for reproduction and nutrition will be affected. Changes in ocean currents could have serious consequences for mankind, as currents play a key role in regulating Earth's climate. Changing these currents will have huge consequences for the global climate, including changes in rainfall, with more rain in some locations and much less in others due to differences in air temperatures. Coral reef and shellfish disruption and destruction will have far-reaching consequences for humanity, resulting in less food for those who rely on the ocean for their food.

CHAPTER 5
Solving the Ocean's Climate Problem

Climate change poses a major threat to marine life, including coral reefs and fisheries, with ramifications for marine ecosystems, economies, and societies, particularly those most reliant on natural resources. Limiting global warming to no more than 1.5°C can lessen the risk posed by climate change. Oceans span more than two-thirds of the earth, yet they haven't gotten their due in terms of research resources or public attention. As a result, the threats that climate change poses to the seas, as well as the remedies that they provide, are frequently disregarded. The ocean is necessary for life on land: it produces half of the world's oxygen and supports the water cycle that provides freshwater, and more than three billion people worldwide rely on fish as a primary protein source. Out of sight and out of mind is the ocean. Today, we believe it is simpler to touch and count trees than fish, but the ocean is what makes the globe habitable.

Climate change is wreaking havoc on ecosystems, businesses, and cultures, particularly those that rely heavily on natural resources. Climate change impacts, on the other hand, can be greatly mitigated if the world as a whole takes steps to keep global warming below 1.5 degrees Celsius. Ocean acidification is caused by the presence of more dissolved carbon dioxide in seawater. Human activities have non-climatic consequences as well, such as overfishing and pollution. If a significant effort is not taken to limit future climate change, the repercussions for human society could be severe.

Because of human-caused climate change, life in most of the world's oceans, from pole to pole and from the sea surface to the abyssal depths, is already experiencing rising temperatures. In many cases, the growth may be imperceptible. Warming has already had severe effects on marine creatures, plants, and bacteria in some areas, particularly near-surface waters. Ocean deoxygenation occurs when less oxygen is accessible due to closely connected changes in seawater chemistry.

Warm-water coral reefs are vital for tropical fisheries and other marine and human systems because they support a diverse range of marine species. They are especially vulnerable because when water temperatures rise above a threshold of 1°C–2°C above usual, they might die in large numbers. Between 2015 and 2017, such conditions occurred in many tropical waters, resulting in widespread coral bleaching as coral animal hosts evicted the algae partners on which they rely. Reef regeneration takes at least 10 to 15 years after mass coral mortality due to bleaching.

Coral habitats can also be found in deeper oceans and cooler seas, and further research is needed to determine how these reefs are affected. Although these cold water corals are not at risk of bleaching, they may weaken or dissolve as a result of ocean acidification and other ocean changes due to their cooler environment. Tropical fisheries could lose up to half of their current catch levels by the end of the century due to high levels of climate change. Because fish populations that are now depleted by overfishing and susceptible to other stressors may not be capable of moving to Polar Regions, as expected in models, polar catch levels may increase marginally, albeit the magnitude of such gains is uncertain.

CHAPTER 6
CLIMATE CHANGE AND THE OCEAN

The ocean covers 71% of the earth and provides a wide range of benefits to human communities, from reducing weather extremes to producing the oxygen we breathe, from producing food to storing excess carbon dioxide. Increasing greenhouse gas emissions, on the other hand, endangers coastal and marine ecosystems by causing changes in ocean temperature and glacier melting, which impact ocean currents, weather patterns, and sea level. Because the ocean's carbon sink capacity has been exceeded, the ocean's chemistry is changing as a result of our carbon emissions. In fact, over the last two centuries, humanity has increased the acidity of our ocean by 30%.

Climate and the ocean are intricately linked. The ocean, as a large heat and carbon sink, plays a critical role in mitigating climate change. Changes in temperature, currents, and sea level rise all affect the health of marine organisms, nearshore and deep ocean ecosystems, and the ocean bears the brunt of climate change. The interrelationship between the ocean and climate change must be recognized, understood, and incorporated into political policies as worries about climate change grow. The amount of carbon dioxide in our atmosphere has increased by approximately 35% since the

Industrial Revolution, owing mostly to the burning of fossil fuels. Ocean waters, ocean species, and ocean habitats all contribute to the ocean absorbing a major percentage of human-caused carbon dioxide emissions.

Climate change and its consequences are already having a substantial impact on the world's oceans. Warming of the air and water, seasonal shifts in species, coral bleaching, sea level rise, coastal inundation, coastal erosion, toxic algal blooms, hypoxic or dead zones, novel marine diseases, the extinction of marine mammals, changes in precipitation levels, and fishery reductions are among them. We can also expect more extreme weather occurrences, such as floods, droughts, storms, and a variety of other unforeseen catastrophes, all of which have an impact on habitats and species. We must take action to conserve our valuable marine habitats.

The overall solution to climate change is to drastically reduce greenhouse gas emissions. The carbon dioxide collected by the world's oceans and coastal ecosystems is known as blue carbon. Blue carbon may be a viable option for long-term carbon sequestration and storage. Carbon is stored in mangroves, tidal marshes, and seagrass meadows in the form of biomass and sediments.

Additional risks must be avoided, and our marine ecosystems must be managed with care, for the sake of the health of the ocean, humans, and animals. We can also boost the resilience of ocean organisms and ecosystems by lowering the acute pressures caused by excessive human activity. We may invest in the ocean's health and immune system in this way by eliminating or minimizing the multiplicity of minor diseases that it faces. Restoring the quantity of ocean species such as mangroves, seagrass meadows, corals, kelp forests, fisheries, and all other ocean life will help the ocean continue to supply the services that all life relies on.

The Basics: The consequences of more powerful storms and increasing sea levels are intangible and will become impossible to ignore. Coastal storms and rising seas will inevitably cause damage, property loss, and infrastructure failures. Although the majority of people now believe in climate change, surveys show that people are more concerned about issues that affect their daily life, such as jobs, health care, drugs, and so on. Though, in the last five years, as people have experienced rising temperatures, more severe storms, and widespread fires, climate change has become a stronger focus. The good news is that there is a rising bottom-up movement for change, and there is greater public awareness than ever before. The Future We Choose is a cautionary tale about two possible futures for the Earth. The first scenario explores what would happen if the Paris Agreement's targets were not realized, while the second scenario considers how the world might look if the carbon emission goals were met. Previous generations lacked this information, and it will be too late for our children, now is the moment to act.

Tipping points, or catastrophes from which the Earth system cannot recover, are more likely than previously thought to occur, resulting in long-term irreversible consequences. The Amundsen Sea in West Antarctica and ice breakdown in the cryosphere may have already crossed their critical thresholds. Other tipping points are also approaching, such as deforestation in the Amazon and bleaching occurrences on Australia's Great Barrier Reef. More research is needed to better understand the alterations that have been noticed, as well as the possibility of cascading consequences. Before the Earth reaches a point of no return, now is the moment to act. In order to limit carbon emissions, a price on carbon is required. A carbon price is a fee levied on companies that emit greenhouse gases in order to shift the expense of climate change from society to the companies that cause it while simultaneously providing an incentive to reduce emissions. To achieve long-term effects, further policies and programs to promote innovation and make low-carbon options more economically appealing are also required. The concept of Blue Carbon, which states that coastal vegetated ecosystems generate disproportionately significant amounts of global carbon sequestration, is crucial to international climate change mitigation and adaptation.

Climate change is a complicated subject that is causing a slew of changes around the planet; it has wreaked havoc on the structure and function of marine ecosystems, in particular. Postglacial rebound, changes in Atlantic Ocean circulation, and the melting of the Antarctic Ice Sheet are all likely contributors to sea-level rise variations. The issue of a warming ocean is a complex one with numerous consequences, some of which may be positive, but the vast majority of which will be harmful in ways that are still unknown. Marine organisms are reacting in predictable ways to the consequences of greenhouse gas emissions and climate change. Poleward and deeper distributional shifts, calcification decreases, increasing abundance of warm-water species, and the loss of entire ecosystems such as coral reefs are some of the responses.

Sea-level rise and coastal erosion have resulted in the loss of the Solomon Islands. This was the first scientific proof of climate change's impact on coastlines and people. Wave energy is thought to have had a key part in the island's erosion. Another nine reef islands have been severely degraded and are on the verge of disappearing in the future years. The ocean's physics, chemistry, ecosystem, and services have all had to change dramatically. Current emissions forecasts would have a rapid and considerable impact on ecosystems that humans rely on extensively. As the ocean continues to warm and acidify as a result of climate change, management options for dealing with the changing ocean become more limited.

The critical function performed by the oceans in climate change is the mixing of heat anomalies into the deep layers. The atmosphere drives the ocean, and ocean circulation is a reaction to atmospheric forcing, such as wind stress, heat fluxes, and moisture fluxes. However, due to intensive sea surface heat exchanges, the ocean exerts the biggest feedback on atmospheric dynamics in the tropical/equatorial zones.

Climate change and global warming affect all aspects of the earth system, including the atmosphere, oceans, land, biosphere, and cryosphere. Because of the immense difficulties of penetrating the deep layers, which are still mostly devoid of observations, and the scarcity of data in the Southern Ocean, the oceans are among the least well-known and understood. Jumping in the ocean is one of the best ways to cool yourself on a hot day. However, in the face of rising global temperatures, marine species do not have it easy. In fact, according to a new study, marine species is more vulnerable to high heat than land animals.

Animals can survive with strong heat waves by finding shade or burrowing underground, depending on where they dwell. On land, it's far easier to escape a heatwave than it is in the sea. Marine species have been harmed worse by extinctions than terrestrial species in several cases. The need for oxygen increases as the temperature rises, and this is likely a factor in increasing marine mortality rates. Marine species are expanding their historical ranges twice as fast as land-based species. Marine animals invade new areas more quickly than terrestrial species. Migration is easier in the ocean than on land, where species may be restricted by terrain or water supply.

When it comes to temperature and oxygen levels, eggs and larvae are generally the most sensitive. Understanding which life phases, species, and ecosystems will be the most severely impacted by climate change will be critical in guiding conservation and management activities as the climate change process progresses.

CHAPTER 7
POLLUTION IN THE OCEAN

Pesticide and fertilizer runoff are causing massive oxygen-depleted dead zones in which many marine creatures are struggling to live. Because oil spills and other forms of pollution at sea account for such a small percentage of total ocean pollution, they have devastating implications. Land-based activities such as sewage, industrial and agricultural runoff, waste dumping, and chemical spills account for over half of all ocean pollution. Another third comes from contaminants in the air, such as sulfur dioxide and mercury, emitted by coal-fired power plants.

Plastics: A rubbish whirlpool floating in the Pacific waters is roughly the size of a state in the United States. The ocean environment is being jeopardized by plastic debris and trash floating around the ocean's coast. Pollution in the form of plastic comes in various shapes and sizes. Hundreds of different marine creatures are choking on smaller particles like the microbeads in your toothpaste and cosmetics. Another big source of pollution in our oceans is plastic. About 10 million metric tons of the 100 million metric tons of plastic produced each year end up in the oceans.

Environmental Harm: Plastic contamination in our environment has been increasingly noticeable in recent years. Its global abundance, distribution, and indications of ecological impact have been the focus of the science behind it. Plastic degradation and breakdown are a previously unknown source of greenhouse gases that is predicted to grow in the future, especially as more plastic is manufactured and accumulates in the environment. Plastic that is not submerged in water and is exposed to direct sunlight produces more gases. These emissions will continue to rise as the amount of plastic in the oceans and on land grows. Human activities have disrupted natural current action and sedimentation patterns; impaired water quality by adding surplus nutrients, toxins, and sediments into coastal waters as a result of nonpoint and point-source pollution; and impacted other physical, chemical, and biological processes.

Ocean Acidification: As our oceans absorb carbon dioxide, they become increasingly acidic. The same greenhouse gases that cause climate change are wreaking havoc on the seas. Every species that lives in the ocean is threatened, especially sensitive coral and numerous forms of plankton, which form the foundation of the food chain.

CHAPTER 8
PROTECTING OUR OCEAN

Habitat preservation is critical for biodiversity conservation. Wild species habitat conservation is one of the most pressing environmental challenges today, both on land and at sea. Land use grows as human populations grow, and wild creatures have fewer places to call home. Human activity has affected more than half of the Earth's terrestrial surface, leading to massive deforestation, erosion and loss of topsoil, biodiversity loss, and extinction. Species cannot exist outside of their natural habitat, such as in a zoo or aquarium, without human intervention. Because they live in multiple natural habitats, migratory species are particularly sensitive to habitat degradation. This necessitates not only the preservation of the two habitats for migratory species but also the preservation of their migratory route. Even little changes to a natural habitat can have a cascading impact that damages the entire ecosystem. Most habitats and ecosystems have inputs and outputs that are related to other habitats and ecosystems.

In the marine environment, habitat degradation is a major issue. The following points discussed in this chapter of the book harm habitats:

Destructive Fishing Practices: Bottom trawling and dynamiting coral reefs are destructive fishing practices that destroy entire ecosystems. Fishing activities are no longer viable; in some locations, fishermen have turned into capitalists that exploit ocean resources for profit. Today, destructive fishing practices are on the rise; we must fish in environmentally friendly methods to protect our planet.

Pollution: Industrial chemicals, insecticides, and motor oil contaminate the ocean as a result of development near coastal waterways. Because pollution is extremely harmful to our ocean, we must protect it from all types of pollutants in order to minimize the negative effects of global warming.

Coastal Development: When marshes are dredged for real estate development, habitats are destroyed. Excess nutrients from fertilizers and domestic sewage are released via soil runoff and erosion, resulting in toxic algae blooms that block sunlight and deplete oxygen levels in the water. It also causes silt to accumulate on coral reefs, obstructing the sunlight required for coral growth.

Dredging: Some business activities in the ocean have major negative consequences. Dredging has the potential to harm seagrass beds and other habitats that offer food, shelter, and breeding grounds for fish. The majority of accumulated silt and contaminants settle below the ocean's surface and into the water. Dredged debris must be disposed of, but it is frequently thrown into salt marshes, causing significant damage to highly productive maritime environments.

Despite the fact that habitat damage has been on the rise for many years, marine habitat protection has only lately been a priority for conservation initiatives, local and national governments, and international marine conservation organizations. The idea of the ocean's invulnerability to human activities is finally being debunked. Coastal regions are still under strong strain from rapidly growing coastal populations, but there are remedies available to avert additional damage. Pollution, commercial fishing equipment, coastal development, and other human activities are responsible for the majority of marine habitat loss. Simple actions can prevent a lot of it.

With the following suggestions, the ocean habitat may be kept safe; these solutions are a fantastic method to keep the oceans clean and flourishing:

Monitoring and Reporting: Some conservation projects are entrusting residents with the task of monitoring water quality in their coastal towns through sampling and testing, documenting polluted areas, and informing local policymakers.

Land Use and Development Regulation: To conserve coastal areas, an integrated strategy to land use and management based on scientific understanding is required. Through easily accessible and evidence-based information, policymakers must be informed about the impact of coastal development on marine habitats.

Marine Reserves: Marine areas where fishing, mineral mining, and other habitat-altering activities are prohibited, providing a higher level of environmental protection. Marine Reserves are significantly more effective than MPAs, however, they aren't as widely used.

Zoning: One major solution we can consider to save the planet is zoning coastal areas into MPAs, Marine Reserves, and approved fishing areas, with varying levels of use, which has the ability to prevent some of the habitat deterioration caused by development. This is how the Great Barrier Reef is handled. This method could provide a feasible solution for all stakeholders, from tourism to the fishing sector to conservation efforts, if local, state, and national governments work together.

CONCLUSION

Oceans are treated as if they don't exist, despite the fact that they encompass 70% of the earth. All they've done is feed us, give the majority of the oxygen we breathe, and protect us from ourselves. Climate change would have already rendered Earth uninhabitable if it weren't for the oceans.

Understand the change: Temperature, moisture, oxygen concentration, and sunlight are all factors that contribute to life on Earth. Understanding current and future climate shifts require unravelling past climatic changes.

Protect the Ocean's Diversity: Warmer waters produce coral bleaching, which has an impact on coral reef ecosystems, which are home to the majority of the ocean's biodiversity and provide vital food supplies for humans.

Reduce global warming: Climate change threatens ecosystems' ability to cope with extreme occurrences and disturbances like wildfires, floods, and drought. When we are intentional in our aspirations towards sustainable living, we may reduce both carbon dioxide and pollution.

www.ingramcontent.com/pod-product-compliance
Lightning Source LLC
Chambersburg PA
CBHW070906220526
45466CB00005B/2140